I0489521

A Coloring Book for Adults

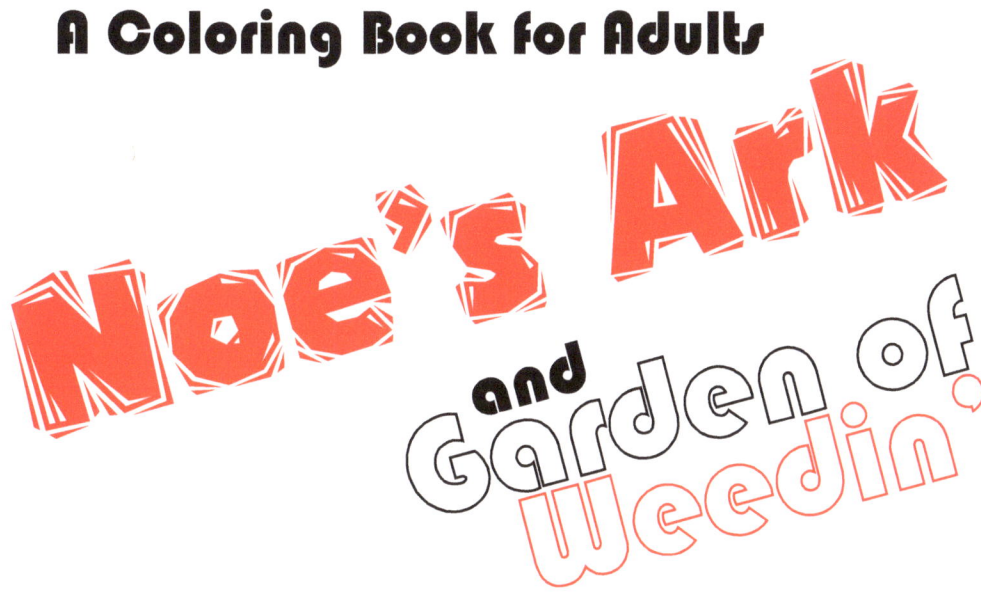

Noe's Ark and Garden of Weedin'

Rita Noe's penchant for puns and word play led to the title of this book. In the King James Version of the Bible, Noah is spelled Noe in five places: Matt. 24:37, Matt. 24:38, Luke 3:36, Luke 17:26, and Luke 17:27. And of course, the theme is flora and fauna.

Why another coloring book for adults?

It's for those who would prefer a more personal viewpoint of the world rather than generic designs. It's for those who need some extra help in creating a balanced composition. It's for those who like detail but sometimes want to color outside the lines. It's for those who want to choose their own colors and medium. (The color photos included on each page are for the purpose of seeing the subject matter more easily. They are not intended as rules for color use.)

Each coloring page is perforated for easy removal to allow the colorist to mat and/or frame the finished work. Permission is granted to frame the page with or without the photo image and text.

Happy coloring!

Copyright © 2016 by Rita Noe. 734333

ISBN: Softcover   978-1-5144-6983-5
        EBook   978-1-5144-6982-8

All rights reserved. No part of this book may
be reproduced or transmitted in any form or by
any means, electronic or mechanical, including
photocopying, recording, or by any information storage
and retrieval system, without permission in writing from
the copyright owner.

Print information available on the last page

Rev. date: 02/25/2016

To order additional copies of this book, contact:
Xlibris
1-888-795-4274
www.Xlibris.com
Orders@Xlibris.com

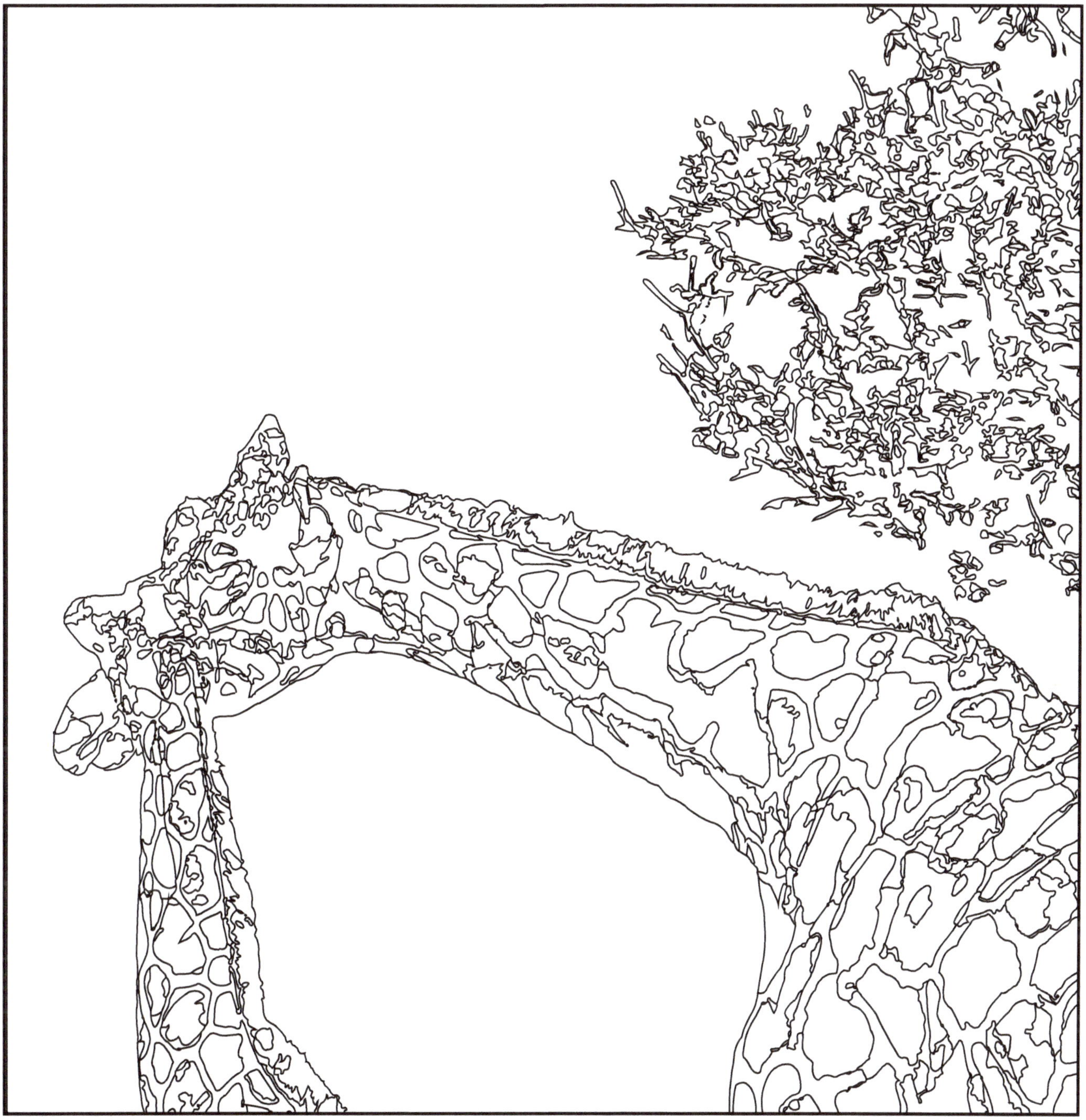

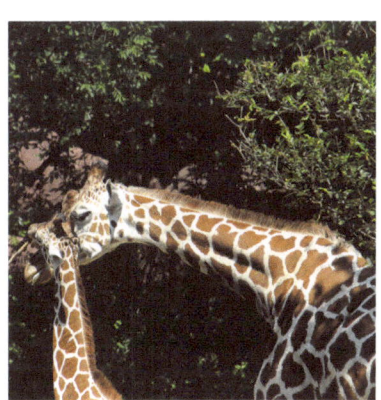

Ahh, Mom!

What could be any more delightful than a gangly, wobbly baby giraffe? St. Louis Zoo, St. Louis, Missouri, USA. © Rita J Noe 2009

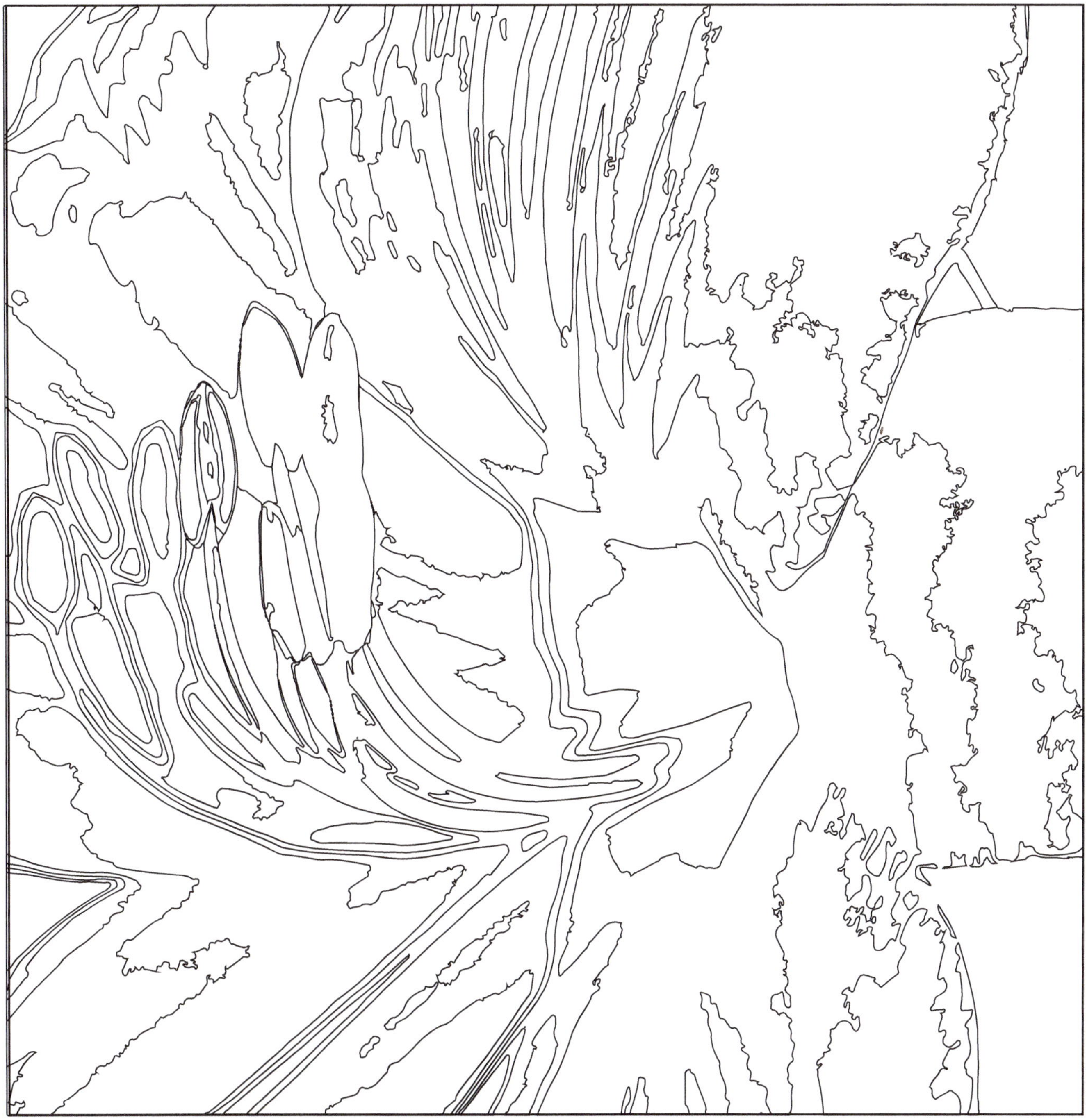

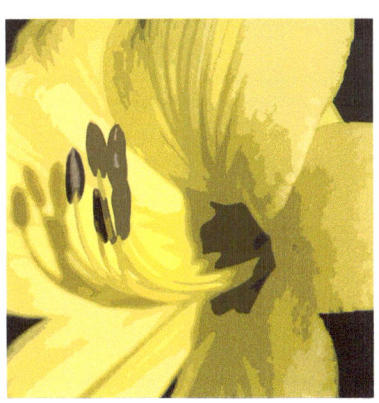

Yellow Sunshine

A trip to the Botanical Gardens in St. Louis started
a love affair with daylilies, like this yellow one.
Keokuk, Iowa, USA. © Rita J Noe 2009

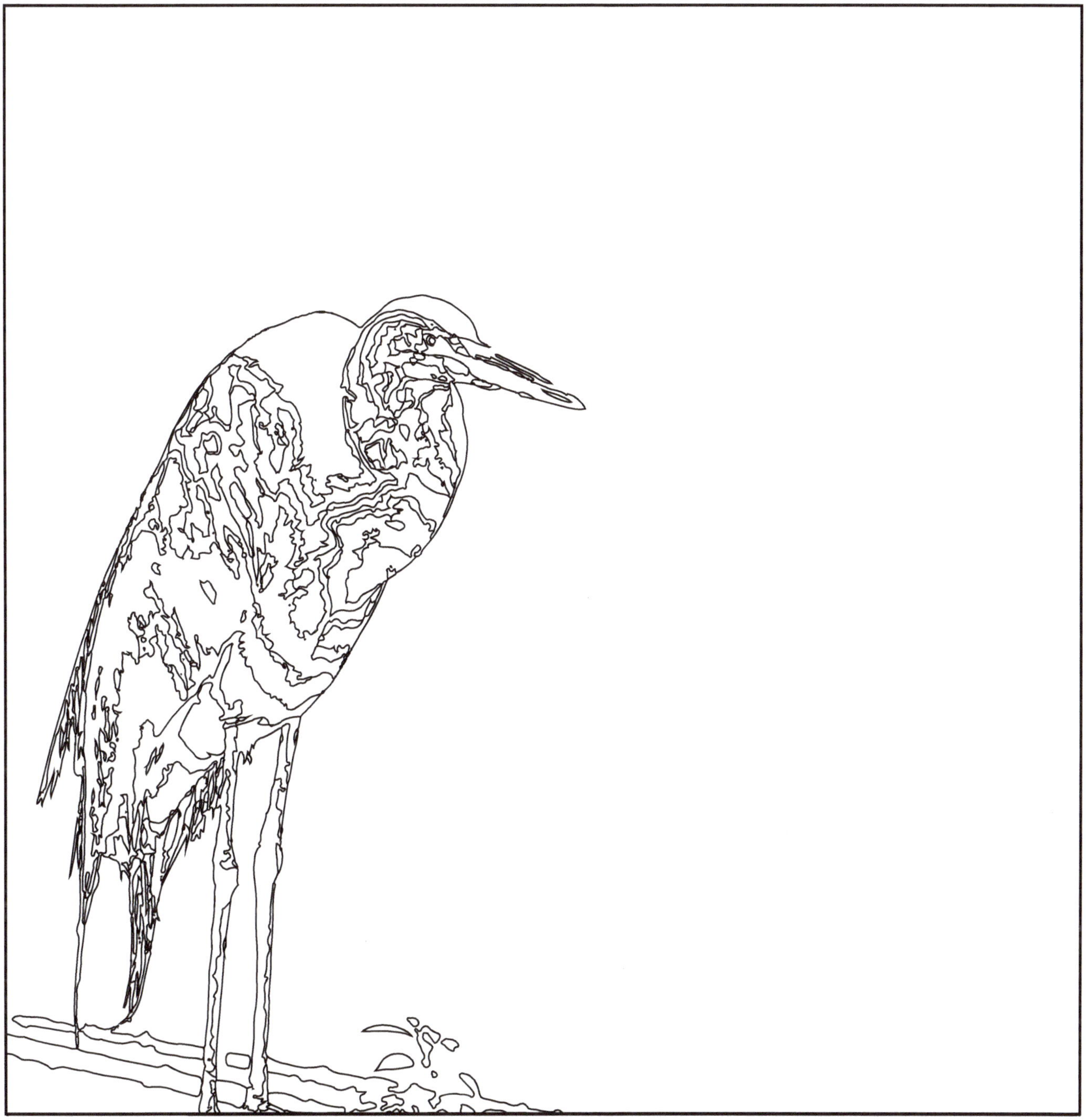

Angst-free Egret

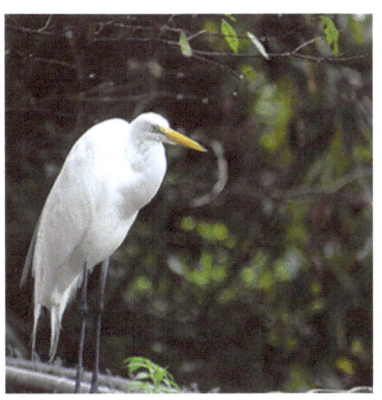

Appearing to have no cares in the world, this egret at Manatee Park in Homosassa, Florida, USA, patiently waits for the next tidbit to make its appearance.
© Rita J Noe, 2007

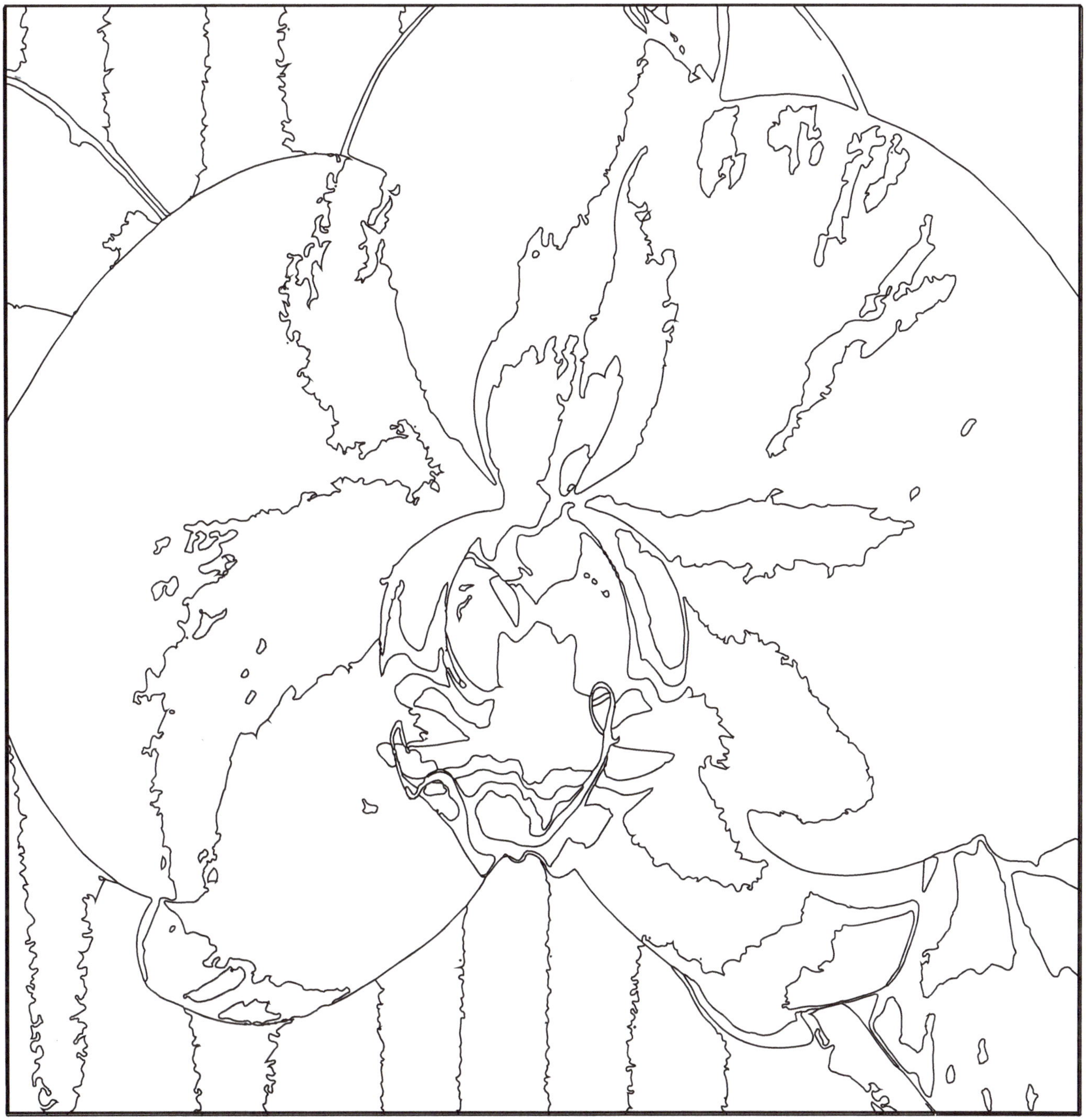

Unfailing Phaelenopsis

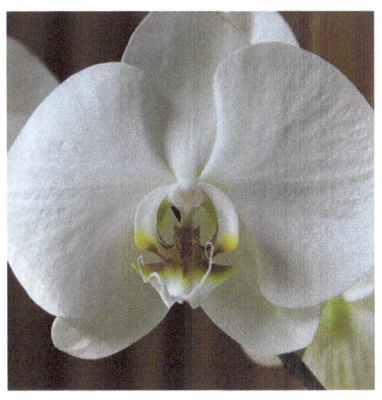

The Phaelenopsis or Moth Orchid is a sculptural, architectural wonder and delight, and never fails to amaze, especially when it blooms for the fifth time. Keokuk, Iowa, USA.
© Rita J Noe 2007

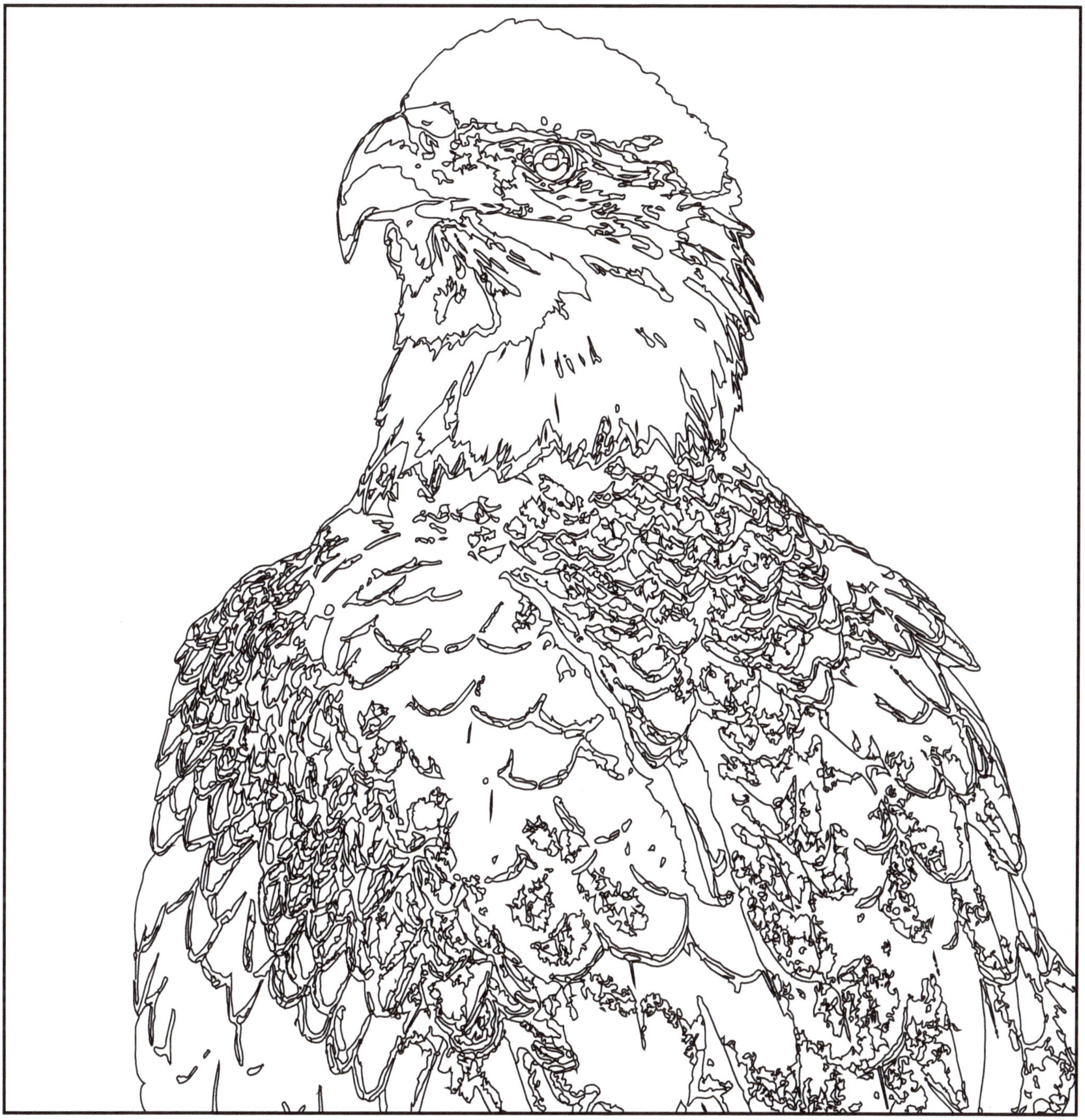

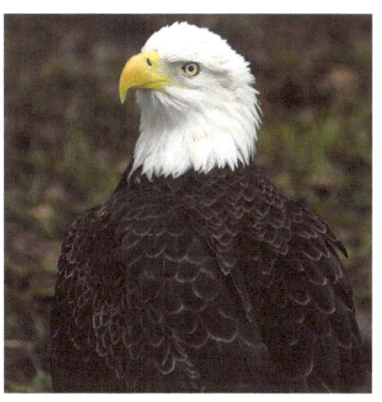

The Old Eagle Eye

Majestic whether in captivity or soaring in the wild,
the American Bald Eagle lives up to its designation
as the symbol of American freedom. Manatee Park,
Homosassa Springs, Florida, USA. © Rita J Noe 2007

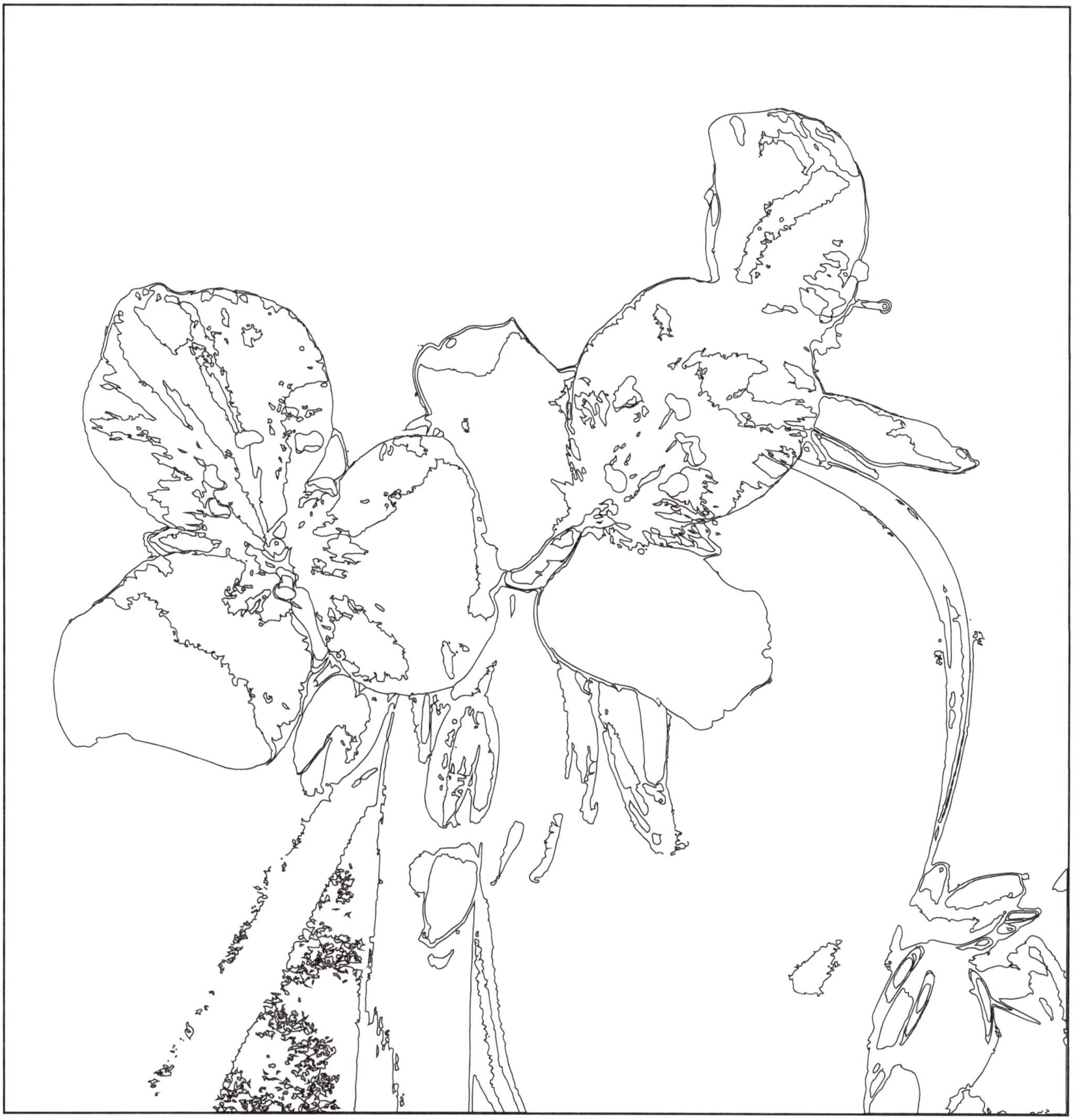

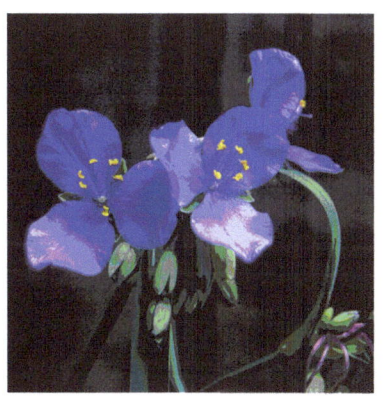

Spiderworts and All

A woodlands delight in the spring in terms of color and its simplicity of three petals, the Spiderwort is considered by some to be a weed. Keokuk, Iowa, USA.

© Rita J Noe 2007

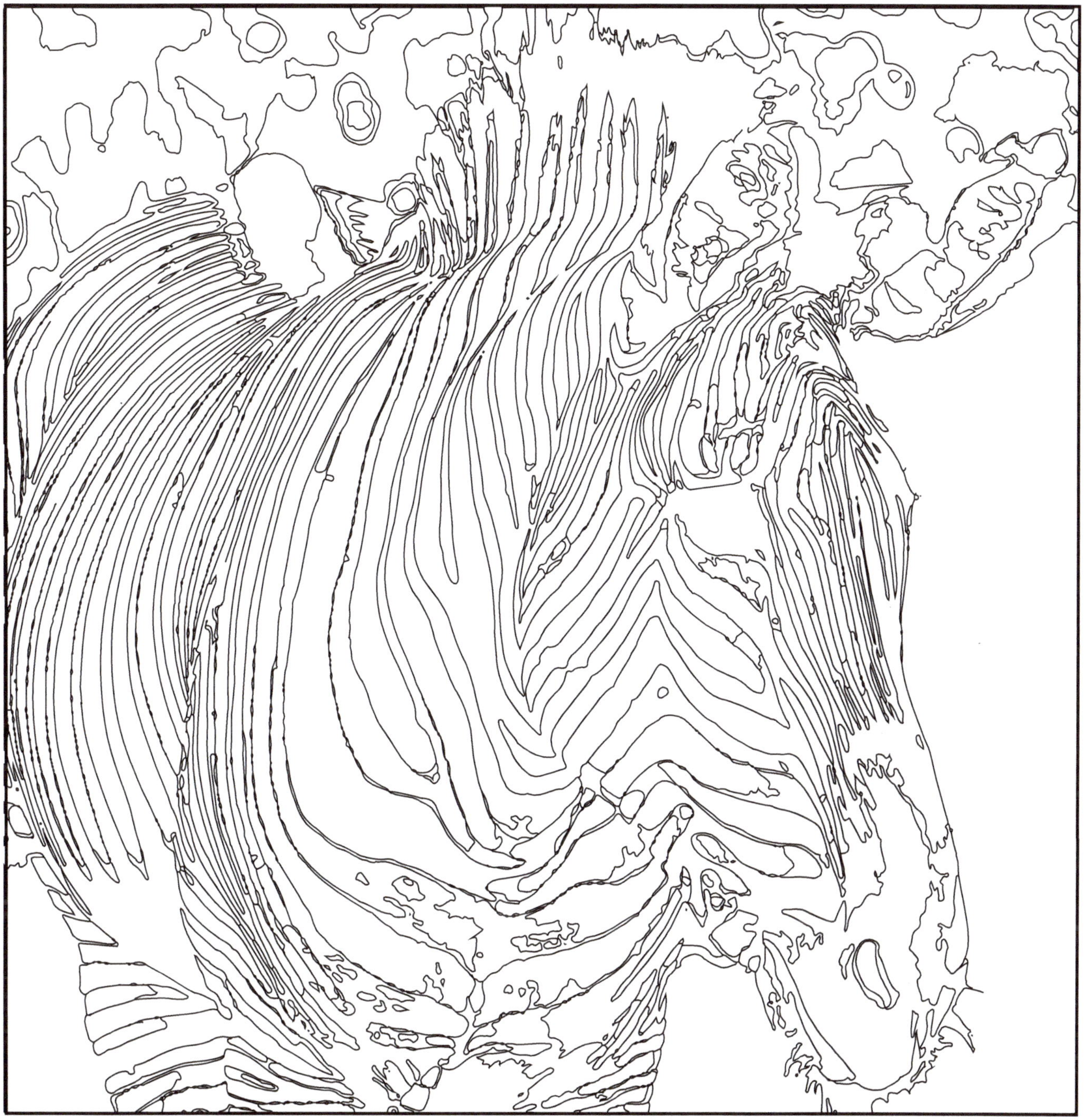

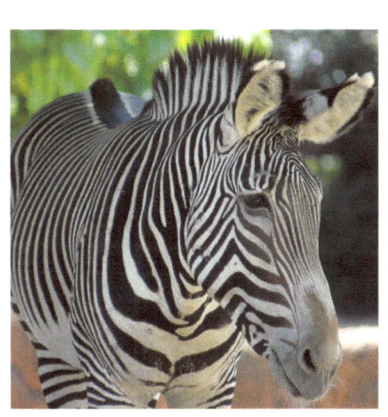

Motion Dazzler

What's black-and-white and red all over? An embarrassed zebra. This one at the St. Louis Zoo doesn't appear to be, just bearing up under a hot humid summer day. St. Louis, Missouri, USA.
© Rita J Noe 2011

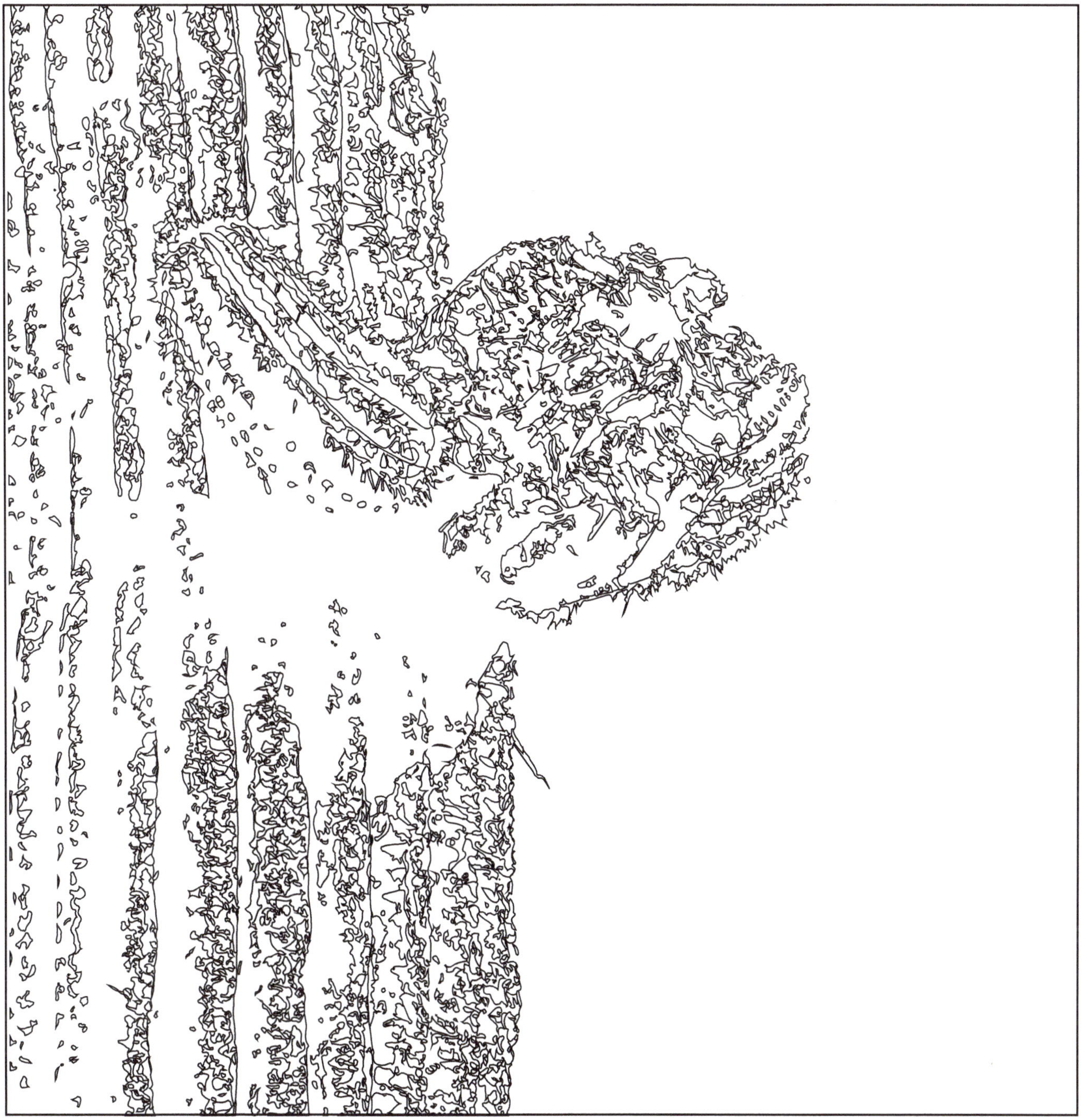

Sonoran Longhorn

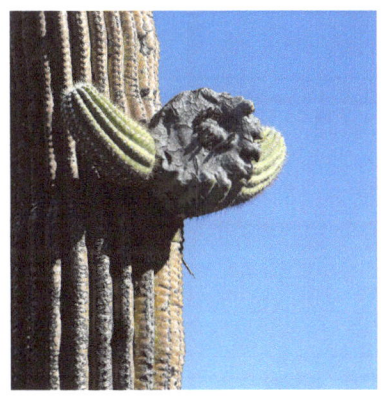

The ubiquitous saguaros of the Sonoran Desert in Arizona are the source of many giggles and outright laughter. Saguaro National Park, Arizona USA.
© Rita J Noe 2013

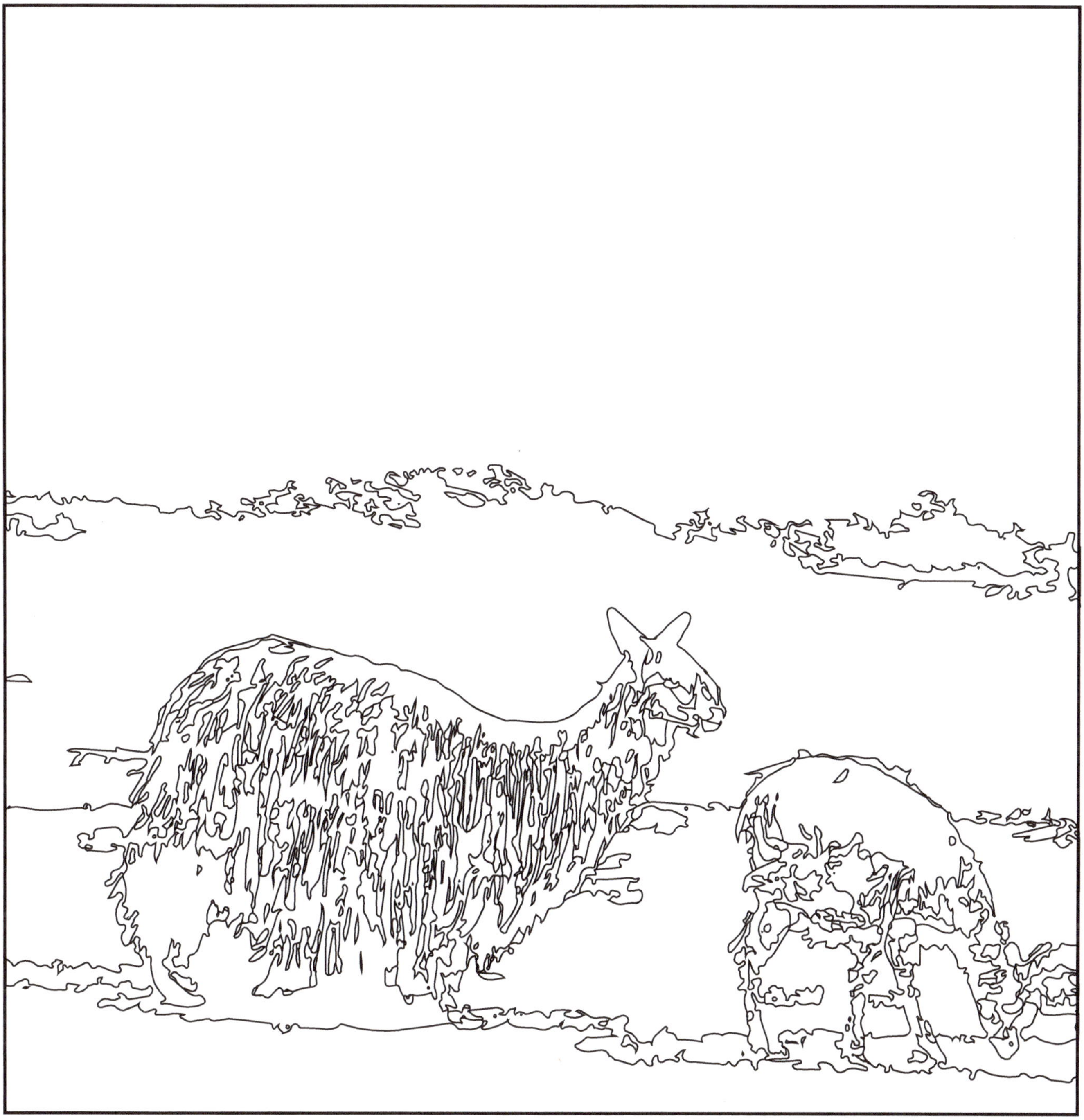

Mama Llama and Her Cria

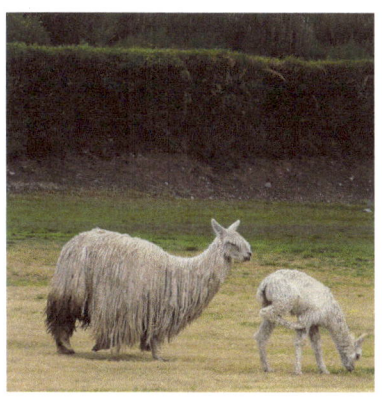

Lama Glama in Quechuan, Yama in Spanish, or
llama in English, this versatile camelid of Peru
supplies meat, wool, and labor for the people.
Ayetaytombo, Peru. © Rita J Noe 2014

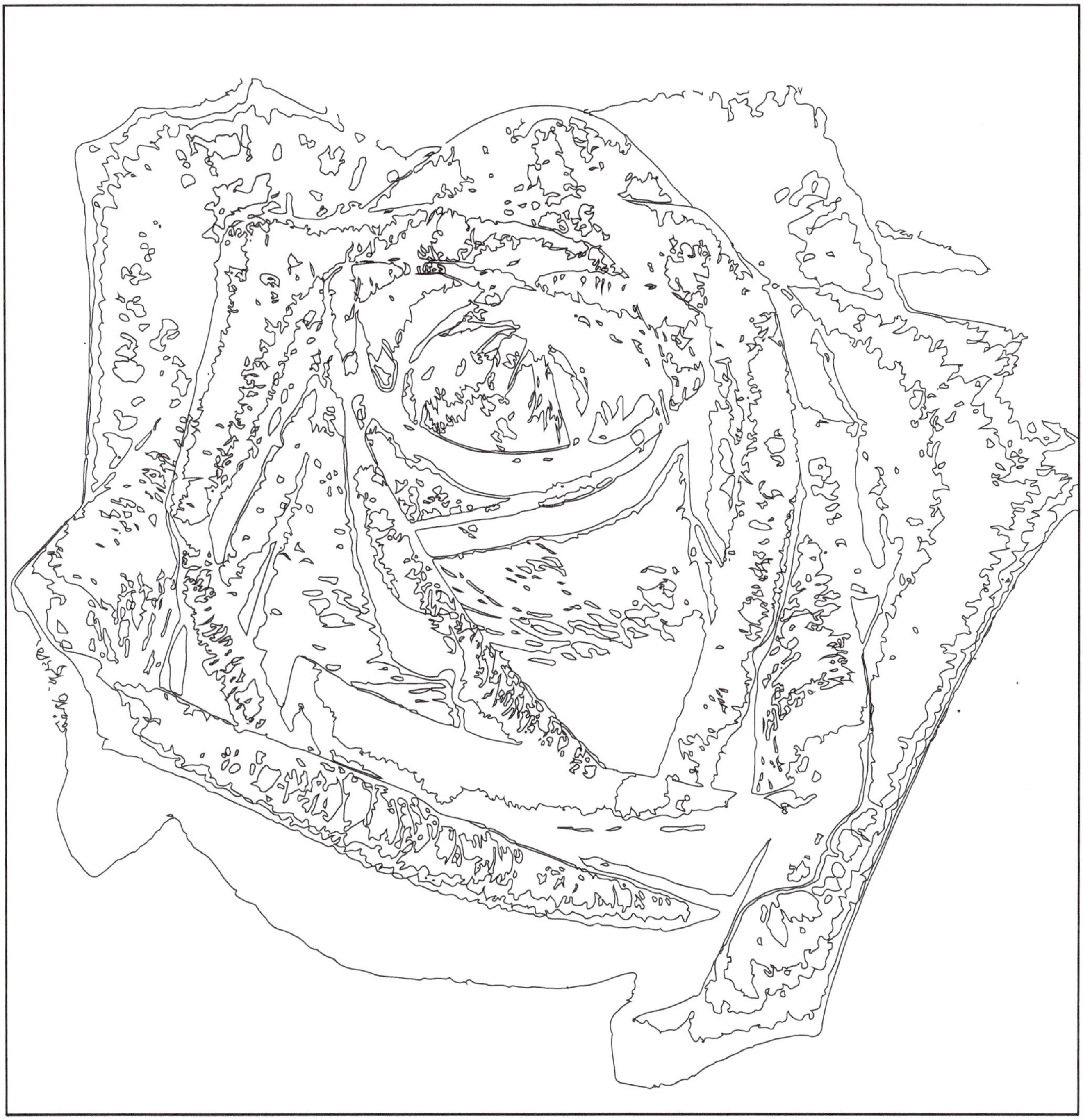

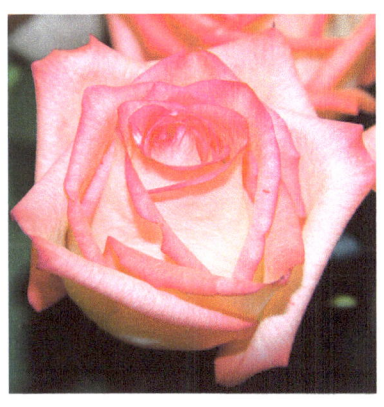

Rosa "Madame A. Meilland" (Peace Rose)

Named at the end of World War II and celebrated at the inaugural meeting of the United Nations in San Francisco (1945), this Chicago Peace Rose variety embodies the spirit of world peace. Rio Rancho, New Mexico, USA. © Rita J Noe 2015

www.ingramcontent.com/pod-product-compliance
Lightning Source LLC
Chambersburg PA
CBHW050438180526
45159CB00006B/2590